Contents

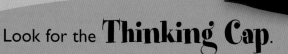

Look for the **Thinking Cap**.
When you see this picture, you will find
a problem to think about and write about.

The three musketeers

Friends forever

Sophie, Nadira and Yasmine had been best friends since their very first week at school. Now that they were twelve years old, they were in their second year at a collège, or high school, in Lyon, France. The other students in their class called the girls 'the three musketeers'. This was because they were very close friends, just like the three characters from the famous French classic *The Three Musketeers* by Alexandre Dumas. The storybook motto, 'One for all, and all for one', applied to these girls as much as it did to the book's characters.

When Nadira was eleven years old, she started wearing a headscarf to school. Recently, Yasmine started wearing one too. Both girls are Muslim, and many Muslim women wear such a head covering to be **modest**. When the girls first started covering their heads, they felt a little embarrassed. It took Sophie a while to get used to her friends dressing differently from her. But all three girls got used to the scarves and no longer paid much attention to them. The girls were still the three musketeers, and they still sat together in class and spent every lunch break together.

modest not revealing or seeking attention in any way

4

Freedom
Debate

France

My name is Suzette. I live in Paris. At my school, there are students from more than 30 different cultures. Some of my Muslim friends wear a headscarf outside of school. They put on the headscarf when they leave the school grounds. To me, it doesn't matter what someone wears. What do you think?

The new law

On 15 March 2004, a new law was passed in France. The girls' teacher explained it to the class. She said that beginning next September, it would be illegal to wear **conspicuous** religious clothing to a government-run school such as theirs. She explained that large Christian crosses, Jewish skullcaps and Muslim headscarves would be banned at the next school year. She said that according to French law there could be no mixing of religion with government. This meant that religion and things connected with religion were not permitted on school grounds.

'That's not fair,' said Jacob Levin. 'My family is Jewish. All the men wear skullcaps. We're proud to wear them. How can the government tell us what to wear?'

conspicuous standing out and easy to see

In 1905, France passed a law separating church and state. Since then, government-run schools have been banned from teaching or promoting any religion.

Nadira and Yasmine exchanged worried glances. What would happen? They knew their parents wanted them to wear the headscarves. Nadira spoke up. 'What difference does it make to anyone else if I wear a headscarf?' she asked.

'The government is worried that you might be treated differently from other students,' their teacher explained. 'Also, if some students wear a headscarf others might feel they have to also.'

'I don't care what anyone else wears,' replied Nadira. 'I'm not pressuring anyone.'

News for Nadira

Over the next few weeks, people discussed the new law at home and wherever they met. There were many hot debates about whether it was right or wrong. One day, Nadira came to school with red eyes. She seemed quiet and sad.

At lunchtime, Sophie and Yasmine asked her what was wrong. 'My parents insist that I must wear the headscarf,' she said.

'But you said that you were happy to wear it,' replied Sophie. 'Have you changed your mind?'

'No, no, it's not that,' answered Nadira, starting to sob. 'They are going to send me to a private Muslim school next year. I'm allowed to practise **hijab** there. Dad says that our religion is more important than my attending this school. We won't be together any more. There'll be no more three musketeers!'

hijab the Muslim practice of covering up, especially wearing a headscarf

Yasmine and Sophie were upset. They had assumed that the three friends would go through high school together. They started to cry too.

'What about you, Yasmine?' asked Sophie. 'Are you staying or going?'

'I'm staying,' replied Yasmine. 'My parents aren't happy about the law, but they want me to blend into the French culture. Also, it may be easier for me to get a good job later on if I don't always wear a headscarf. Some people are **prejudiced** against Muslims.'

Not all Muslim women follow the same dress code. For example, some wear a headscarf, while others wear a full veil over their faces. Others do not practise hijab.

prejudiced having a negative, one-sided opinion of another person or group of people that disregards the other person's/people's rights

9

The two musketeers

On 2 September 2004, when the new school year started in France, Yasmine wore her headscarf right up to the school gate. Then she took it off and put it in her bag. It felt strange to be without it in public.

That morning, a few students made comments. A girl from her class told her that she had pretty hair. One of the girls from a tough **clique** remarked that it was a good thing Yasmine was behaving like a proper French girl now. Yasmine felt uncomfortable. She longed to put the scarf back on. However, by the next day, most students were used to Yasmine's new look, and the subject was pretty much forgotten.

clique group of people that stick together and sometimes exclude others

What was hard to forget was Nadira. Both Yasmine and Sophie
missed her a great deal. They missed her friendly smile and witty sense
of humour. Sophie tried to call Nadira after school on the first day, but
Nadira wasn't home yet. Nadira now had to take a long train ride to and
from her new school. When Nadira called Sophie back later that evening,
she sounded tired and unhappy.

'I miss you and Yasmine,' she said. 'I don't have any friends at my
new school.'

The pact

A month later, it was Sophie's birthday. She invited
Yasmine and Nadira to her apartment for dinner.
It was good to be all together again. The girls were
soon chatting and laughing just like in the old days.

'How's your new school, Nadira?' Yasmine asked.

'It's better now that I'm getting used to it,'
answered Nadira, helping herself to a piece of cake.
'I'm part of a big group of girls who hang out
together. I really like some of them. But no one
is as much fun as you two.'

Yasmine and Sophie were relieved
to hear that. They didn't want to be
replaced too easily.

As the evening wore on, the girls
started talking about what they wanted
to do when they grew up. It turned out
that they all planned to go to a university.

'I know what,' said Sophie. 'Let's all go
to the same university. There are no clothing
rules for universities, so we can all be
together again.'

The others agreed enthusiastically.
They made a **pact** to reunite at university.

'Three cheers for the three musketeers!' they
chorused. Then they clinked their glasses together.

pact formal or an important agreement

Put on your thinking cap

Write down your thoughts about the following questions. Then discuss them with a classmate.

1. Why do you think many French people supported the law banning conspicuous religious symbols?

2. Why do you think other French people were unhappy about the new law?

3. How would you feel if your government passed a law banning the wearing of conspicuous religious items?

What's the issue?

In the past, France was ruled by a monarchy that gave special privileges to the rich and to the Catholic Church. Then, beginning in 1789, France underwent a revolution. Eventually, the country became a republic with the motto 'Liberty, Equality and **Fraternity**'. The French people wanted all citizens to have equal opportunities, no matter what social class or religious group they belonged to. In 1905, France passed a law separating the government from the Catholic Church, which most French people belonged to. Teachers were forbidden to say prayers or discuss religious matters in government-run schools. Then on 2 September 2004, it became illegal to wear conspicuous religious items to government-run schools in France. However, many people felt that this law was unfair. They felt it targeted mainly Muslim women. There was a great deal of debate about whether the law was fair or unfair.

After class, a student at Auguste Blanqui High School in France prepares to put on her outer headscarf.

fraternity group of people with a common purpose or interest like a family

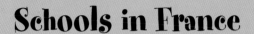
Schools in France

...he US Constitution calls for ...separation of church and state. ...ople observe many different ...ligions in the United States, ...d this law is intended ...ensure religious freedom ...d equality for all.

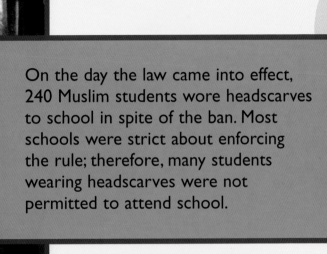

There are three main kinds of schools in France.

1. Government-run schools

2. Private schools that the government helps fund so that they are more affordable. These schools teach the same things as government schools, but many are run by religious groups and have optional religious education classes.

3. Private schools that completely fund themselves and have more choice in what they teach than other schools. Some of these schools are religious. Some are not.

The law banning conspicuous religious symbols applies only to the first kind of school. The other schools have their own rules about dress code.

On the day the law came into effect, 240 Muslim students wore headscarves to school in spite of the ban. Most schools were strict about enforcing the rule; therefore, many students wearing headscarves were not permitted to attend school.

Equality versus rights

In many Western countries, such as France and the United States, most people agree that freedom and equality are important. However, not everyone agrees on how this should work. For example, is it a person's right to wear whatever religious items he or she wants to wear? Or should people dress the same so that no one runs the risk of being victimised or getting special attention because of their beliefs? What about other kinds of clothing? Should some children be allowed to wear clothing associated with gangs to school? Or is this unacceptable because other students might feel threatened? There are no straightforward right or wrong answers, which is why the members of schools, clubs and governments often have fierce debates about what rules or laws should be made.

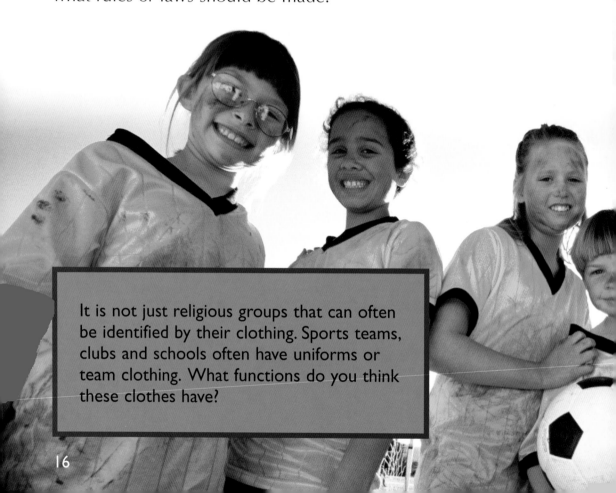

It is not just religious groups that can often be identified by their clothing. Sports teams, clubs and schools often have uniforms or team clothing. What functions do you think these clothes have?

Clothing is often an expression of one's personality. However, some styles of dress can seem threatening to other people. Why do you think some styles of clothing can **intimidate** others?

intimidate to make another person timid or afraid of you

Put on your thinking cap

Write down your thoughts about the following questions. Then discuss them with a classmate.

1. Think about a rule you have to obey. Why do you think this rule was made? Do you agree with this rule? Why or why not?

2. Do you have a dress code at your school? Do you think dress codes are a good or bad idea? Why or why not?

A wider issue

It is not just clothing issues that become discussions for debates about freedom. Other debates involve the issue of whether freedom or safety is more important. For instance, there is debate about whether TV stations should be allowed to show violent programmes. Some people say that violent programmes should be banned because they encourage people to think that violence is okay and to imitate the violence. Others feel that people should be responsible for their own behaviour. They think it is not the network's fault if someone is foolish enough to copy something violent that was shown on television. Even within our homes, issues of freedom versus safety are often debated. Most parents and caregivers create rules to keep their children safe. However, many teens rebel against these rules because they want more freedom.

In the United Kingdom, there is a debate about whether or not people should have to carry identity cards. Some say that this is important for national security. Others say that it would take away people's basic liberty.

During World War II, some Japanese Americans were forced to live in special camps. They lost their freedom because some people thought that they might be enemy spies. Many people said that this loss of freedom was necessary for national security. Others felt that it was unfair.

Is it an issue of women's rights?

Some religions, such as the Amish and Muslim religions, encourage women to dress in ways that cover up much of their bodies. Some people feel that this is unfair to women. They believe that women should have the same freedom as men. However, many French Muslim women feel that practising hijab should be their choice. They say that a law forbidding them to wear a headscarf takes away their freedom just as much as someone telling them that they must wear one.

Clothing rules around the world

Uniform yes, headscarf maybe

UNITED KINGDOM – In England, many government-run schools require students to wear uniforms. Muslim students, however, are usually allowed to wear a headscarf with their school uniform. Jewish students may wear a skullcap, and religious crosses are also permitted.

A right to choose

UNITED ARAB EMIRATES – The official state religion of the United Arab Emirates is Islam. Here some students wear headscarves and others do not. All women, including schoolchildren, are permitted to make the choice for themselves.

Symbols on or off

UNITED STATES – In state schools in the United States students can choose whether or not to wear their religious items. Many Jewish students for example, choose to wear a skullcap.

Uniformity

CANADA AND UNITED STATES –
Some United States and
Canadian children belong to
religious groups, such as the
Amish, that have a dress code
that requires everyone to dress
in a prescribed style. Many of
these children attend private
schools with other children from
the same religious group.

All covered up

IRAN – Iran is a Muslim country.
Iranian law requires all females
over the age of seven to practise a
minimum level of hijab when in
public. Some choose to cover up
even more than this minimum
as a matter of personal choice.
Others wear only what the law
requires.

Dressed in colour

BRAZIL – In the Amazon
rainforest, some children do
not wear as many clothes as
children in Brazilian towns
and cities. Their culture has
a different dress style, and
these children are considered
appropriately dressed.

What's your opinion?

Many of us like to show our personalities by wearing particular clothes. Some kinds of clothes show that we belong to a particular team or club, such as a football team or scouts. Other clothes can be an expression of our **individuality**.

- How important is the issue of clothing to you? Do you think that students should be allowed to wear conspicuous religious items to school? What about other clothing that some people might find offensive or distasteful, such as ripped jeans or very short skirts? Explain your opinion.

- Do you think school uniforms are a good idea? Why or why not? What is the proper balance between individual freedom and school rules?

Some clothing rules have their place. Police officers wear uniforms so people can identify them. I think that school uniforms can be good too, because then poorer kids don't need to worry about buying expensive, designer clothes for school. However, I think kids should be able to wear religious items regardless of whether they have a uniform or not.

individuality qualities that make a person different from others

I think rules have a place. They are usually designed to keep things fair or to keep people safe. We should think about why the rules were made, rather than just rebel against them. It is impossible for any country to allow complete freedom because people would abuse it and could harm themselves or others. The same goes for smaller organisations, such as schools.

I think it is important that everyone is free to dress however he or she wants. It is unfair for someone's personal dislikes to determine how others dress. This is especially so if the rules prevent people from following their religion. Schools should teach us about the adult world, where most people dress however they want. We need to learn to accept the differences of others, not force everyone to be the same.

Think tank

Do your own research at the library, on the Internet, or with a parent or teacher to find out about clothing restrictions and learn abo what people around the world think about this issue.

1. If you moved to another country, what changes would you be prepared to make in the way you dress in order to fit in? What changes would you not be prepared to make? Explain your answer.

2. What are the advantages and the disadvantages of school uniforms?

3. Sometimes one important value or issue, such as equality, may be upheld at the expense of another, such as freedom. Give examples of situations where one value has been made more important than another. Explain your thoughts.

Glossary

clique group of people that stick together and sometimes exclude others

conspicuous standing out and easy to see

fraternity group of people with a common purpose or interest like a family

hijab the Muslim practice of covering up, especially wearing a headscarf

individuality qualities that make a person different from others

intimidate to make another person timid or afraid of you

modest not revealing or seeking attention in any way

pact formal or an important agreement

prejudiced having a negative, one-sided opinion of another person or group of people that disregards the other person's/people's rights